D0623632

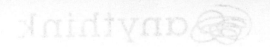

CODE YOUR OWN
KNIGHT ADVENTURE

CODE WITH SIR PERCIVAL
AND DISCOVER THE BOOK OF SPELLS

By Max Wainewright

Quarto is the authority on a wide range of topics.

Quarto educates, entertains and enriches the lives of
our readers—enthusiasts and lovers of hands-on living.

www.quartoknows.com

Author: Max Wainewright
Illustration and design: Henry Smith
Designer: Adrian Morris
Editor: Claudia Martin

This library edition published in 2017 by Quarto Library.,
Part of The Quarto Group
6 Orchard, Lake Forest, CA 92630

Distributed in the United States and Canada by
Lerner Publisher Services
241 First Avenue North
Minneapolis, MN 55401 U.S.A.
www.lernerbooks.com

A CIP record for this book is available from the Library of Congress.

ISBN: 978 1 68297 180 2

Printed in China

Scratch is developed by the Lifelong Kindergarten Group at MIT Media Lab.
See: http://scratch.mit.edu

INTERNET SAFETY

Children should be supervised when using the Internet, particularly when using an unfamiliar website for the first time.
The publishers and author cannot be held responsible for the content of the websites referred to in this book.

INFORMATION ON RESOURCES

You can use Scratch on a PC or Mac by opening your web browser
and going to: http://scratch.mit.edu
Then click "Try it out."

There is a very similar website called "Snap," which also works on iPads.
It is available here: http://snap.berkeley.edu/run

If you want to run Scratch without using the web, you can download it from here:
http://scratch.mit.edu/scratch2download/

CONTENTS

USING SCRATCH

In this book, we will use a computer language called Scratch to code our games. It's free to use and easy to learn. Before you set off on your quest with Sir Percival, take a few minutes to get to know Scratch.

FINDING SCRATCH

To start using Scratch, open up a web browser and click in the address bar. Type in **scratch.mit.edu** then press **"Return."** Click **Try it out**.

STARTING SCRATCH

To code a computer game, you need to tell your computer exactly what to do. You do this by giving it commands. In Scratch, commands are shown in the form of "code blocks." You build a game by choosing code blocks and then joining them together to create a program.

Your Scratch screen should look like this:

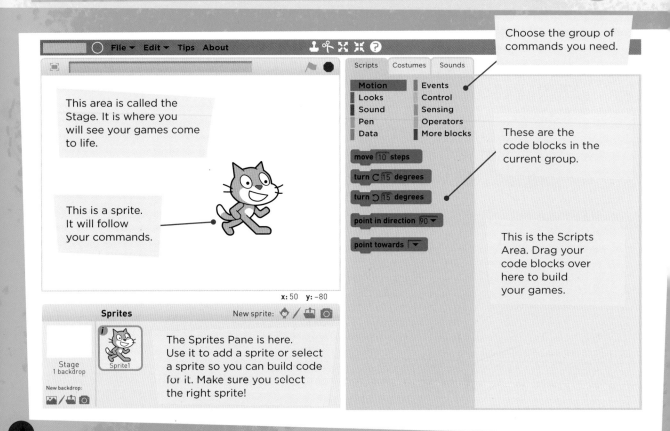

Choose the group of commands you need.

This area is called the Stage. It is where you will see your games come to life.

This is a sprite. It will follow your commands.

These are the code blocks in the current group.

This is the Scripts Area. Drag your code blocks over here to build your games.

The Sprites Pane is here. Use it to add a sprite or select a sprite so you can build code for it. Make sure you select the right sprite!

USING CODE BLOCKS

Before you drag out any code blocks, try clicking on one to make the cat sprite move forward...

...or rotate 15 degrees.

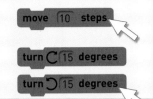

Click in the white boxes (which are shown in this book as colored) then type different numbers to change how far the sprite moves or turns.

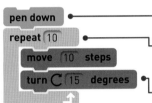

Now try dragging code blocks over to the Scripts Area and joining them together. Click on one of the blocks to run the whole program.

You can break code blocks apart, but you need to start with the bottom block if you want to separate them all. To remove a code block, drag it off the Scripts Area.

Use the color of the code blocks to figure out which group you will find the block in. It will also give you a clue about what the code block will do.

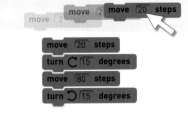

Get the **"Pen down"** block from the green **Pen** group.

The **"Repeat"** block is a mustard color, so it's in the **Control** group.

The blue code blocks are in the **Motion** group.

USING THE DRAWING AREA

To draw a new sprite, click on the **Paint new sprite** button located in the top bar of the **Sprites Pane**.

To draw a backdrop for the Stage, click on the **Stage** button located in the **Sprites Pane** then click on **Paint new backdrop** underneath it.

The **Drawing Area** will appear on the right of your Scratch screen:

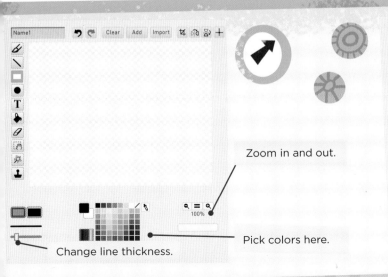

Zoom in and out.

Pick colors here.

Change line thickness.

Brush
Use this tool for drawing.

Rectangle
Draw a rectangle. Hold down the **"Shift"** key to make a square.

Ellipse (Oval)
Draw an ellipse. Hold down the **"Shift"** key to make a circle.

Fill
Fill an area by clicking in it with the mouse.

You receive a note from your old friend Sir Percival. He begs you to meet him at the Great Hall...

Help! Queen Matilda has sent me on a quest. The evil Wizard Malvin has kidnapped her children, Prince George and Princess Georgina, and is holding them prisoner in the Enchanted Castle. Wizard Malvin is the most powerful wizard in the land thanks to his Book of Spells! I need to rescue the prince and princess AND destroy the Book of Spells. P-please, pleeeeease help me with my quest!

Of course you cannot let poor Sir Percival go on his quest alone. But before you set off, you must put on your armor.

KNIGHT TIME

1. Open **Scratch**.

 Let's delete the cat sprite. In the **Sprites Pane**, **right click** the cat.

 On a Mac, hold the **"Ctrl"** key then **click**.

 Choose **Delete**.

2. To start drawing yourself as a knight, click the **Paint new sprite** button in the **Sprites Pane**.

3. Now you should be able to see the **Drawing Area**.

 Choose the **Ellipse** tool.

 At the bottom of the screen, click the **Solid ellipse**.

4. Select a **skin color**.

Draw your head by dragging the mouse.

5. Choose the **Rectangle** tool.

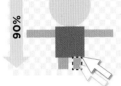

90%

Draw **gray** rectangles for your body, arms, and legs. Your drawing should be **almost as tall** as the Drawing Area. If not, your games might not work.

6. Add more rectangles for your shoes and shield.

 If things go wrong, click **Undo** and go back a step.

7. Choose the **Line** tool.

 Set it to a **medium thickness**.

8. Add a belt, sword, and 2 lines at the bottom of your shield.

9. Choose the **Fill** tool then click in your shield.

10. Use the **Brush** tool to add details.

 Use the other tools to personalize your outfit.

 Use the **Eraser** to round off your shoes.

Turn the page to find out how to save your knight drawing so you can use it on your quest. Turn over right now!

I think I have an idea! Many years ago, a kind fairy gave me a flying carpet. Surely it could come in handy on our quest! Please help me collect it from my cottage.

FIND THE FLYING CARPET

1. Before you do anything else, save your knight sprite so you can use it in all the other activities in this book.

In the **Sprites Pane**, **right click** on the **knight** sprite icon. On a Mac, hold the "Ctrl" key and **click**.

delete

save to local file

Click **Save to local file**.

Type in **knight** as a name for your sprite and click **OK**.

2. In the center of the screen, click the **Scripts** tab so Scratch is ready for you to add some code to make your knight move.

Scripts   Costumes

3. Drag these blocks into the **Scripts Area**, in this order. Remember that the color of each block tells us which group it is in. So the **"When green flag clicked"** block is in the **Events** group. The blue blocks are in the **Motion** group. All the purple blocks are in the **Looks** group. The **"Repeat"** loop block is in **Control**. You can click in the white box in a block in order to change the message or number, so click in the **"Say"** block to type in the words.

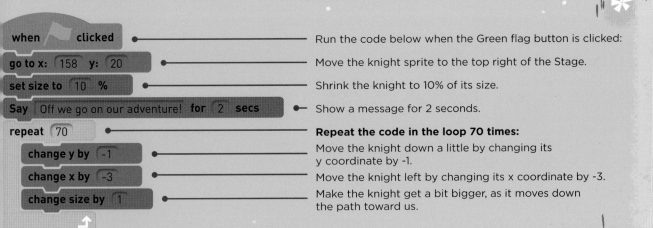

when ⚑ clicked ————————— Run the code below when the Green flag button is clicked:

go to x: 158 y: 20 ————————— Move the knight sprite to the top right of the Stage.

set size to 10 % ————————— Shrink the knight to 10% of its size.

Say Off we go on our adventure! for 2 secs ●— Show a message for 2 seconds.

repeat 70 ————————— **Repeat the code in the loop 70 times:**

　　change y by -1 ————————— Move the knight down a little by changing its y coordinate by -1.

　　change x by -3 ————————— Move the knight left by changing its x coordinate by -3.

　　change size by 1 ————————— Make the knight get a bit bigger, as it moves down the path toward us.

What are coordinates?

The code above uses coordinates to position and move your knight sprite. If you haven't learned about coordinates in school yet, just try experimenting with different numbers and you'll soon figure it out.

The x number gives Scratch the left to right position on the Stage. The y number gives the top to bottom position.

The position x: 0, y: 0 is in the center of the Stage.

4. Now we will create a backdrop for the Stage to show a path through the forest.

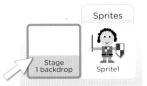

In the **Sprites Pane**, click the **Stage** icon.

Just below, click **Choose backdrop from library**.

Choose **castle3**. Then click **OK**.

5. Click the **Green flag** button at the top right of the **Stage** to test your code. Walk down the path and collect Sir Percival's flying carpet!

To save your code, click the **File** menu, then **Download to your computer**. Then to use it again, click **File** and **Upload from your computer**.

Armed with the flying carpet, you draw near the Enchanted Castle. It lurks at the heart of a very strange forest...

Aaaaargh! These trees are under one of Wizard Malvin's deadly spells!

Leap onto the flying carpet and make your escape from the...

FEARSOME FOREST

1. Start a new Scratch file.

File▼

New

2. In the **Sprites Pane**, **right click** the **cat sprite** icon. On a Mac, hold **"Ctrl"** and **click**.

Click **Delete**.

3. In the center of the screen, click **Backdrops**.

Choose the **Fill** tool.

Choose **dark green**.

Fill the background by clicking in the **Drawing Area**.

4. Choose the **Brush** tool.

Choose **blue**.

Make the brush width **thicker**.

Draw the castle's moat in the **bottom right corner** of the Drawing Area.

5. Zoom in to make it easier to draw the castle.

400%

Click the **Plus** button to zoom in to **400%**.

6. Use the **scroll bars** to move the backdrop over to the bottom right side.

You need to be able to see the moat.

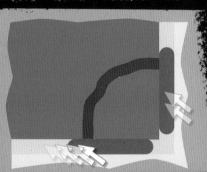

7. Choose the **Rectangle** tool.

Select **dark gray**, then choose the **Solid rectangle**.

8. Draw the Enchanted Castle inside the moat using rectangles.

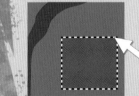

Make sure you draw the entrance to the castle in **black**.

9. In the **Sprites Pane**, click the **Choose sprite from library** button to add a magic tree.

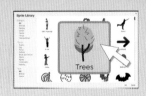

Scroll down then click the **Trees** image.

Click **OK**.

Make sure you use the same tree as this one or your code may not work properly.

10. In the Scratch **Menu bar**, click the **Shrink** button. Now **click** the tree on the **Stage** several times until it is about the same size as the castle.

11. Now upload your **knight** sprite.

In the **Sprites Pane**, click **Upload sprite from file**.

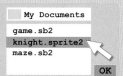
My Documents
game.sb2
knight.sprite2
maze.sb2
OK

Find your file and click **OK**.

The sprite will appear.
Sprite1

---

12. Now let's add your flying carpet.

Click the **Costumes** tab.

Costumes

You may have to zoom back to **100%**.

100%

Use the **Brush** tool to draw the carpet.

Make the brush **thinner** to draw tassles at each end

---

13. Click the **Scripts** tab then drag these blocks into the **Scripts Area**. The **"Touching color"** blocks are in the **Sensing** group. You will need to drop them in the holes in the **"Repeat until"** and **"If then"** blocks.

Scripts

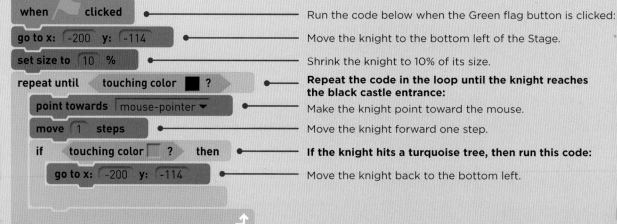

when 🏳 clicked — Run the code below when the Green flag button is clicked:

go to x: -200 y: -114 — Move the knight to the bottom left of the Stage.

set size to 10 % — Shrink the knight to 10% of its size.

repeat until touching color ■ ? — **Repeat the code in the loop until the knight reaches the black castle entrance:**

point towards mouse-pointer ▼ — Make the knight point toward the mouse.

move 1 steps — Move the knight forward one step.

if touching color □ ? then — **If the knight hits a turquoise tree, then run this code:**

go to x: -200 y: -114 — Move the knight back to the bottom left.

say You have reached the castle! — When the knight reaches the castle, show a message.

How to set the color for a "Touching color" block

Click the colored square.

touching color □ ?

The pointer changes.

On the Stage, click the color you want to check for.

The color is now set.

touching color ■ ?

14. Now we'll make more trees.

Right click the tree on the **Stage** and choose **Duplicate**. On a Mac, hold **"Ctrl"** and **click**.

15. Drag the new tree into a space in the forest.

Repeat step 14 to add more trees, but make sure it's possible for the flying carpet to reach the castle.

16. Click the **Green flag** button to practice flying around. Move your **mouse pointer** to make the flying carpet sail toward it. Now fly to the castle!

Remember to save your game by clicking the **File** menu, then **Download to your computer**.

Disaster! The Enchanted Castle is protected by a fire-breathing dragon! Can you escape its scorching flames?

DRAGON TROUBLE

1. Start a new Scratch file and **delete** the **cat sprite**.

2. To create the dragon, click **Choose sprite from library**.

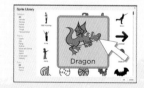 Click the **Dragon** icon.

 OK Click **OK**.

3.  Click **Upload sprite from file** to get your **knight** sprite.

 Find your file and click **OK**.

4.  Draw the **flying carpet** again. See page 12 step 12 for help.

5. Click the **Scripts** tab then drag these blocks into the **Scripts Area** to move the **knight**.

 Scripts

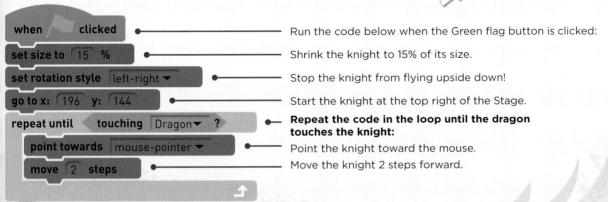

Run the code below when the Green flag button is clicked:

Shrink the knight to 15% of its size.

Stop the knight from flying upside down!

Start the knight at the top right of the Stage.

Repeat the code in the loop until the dragon touches the knight:

Point the knight toward the mouse.

Move the knight 2 steps forward.

6. Now we need to add code to make the dragon move.

Click the **dragon** in the **Sprites Pane**.

 Scripts

Click the **Scripts** tab and drag this code into the **Scripts Area**.

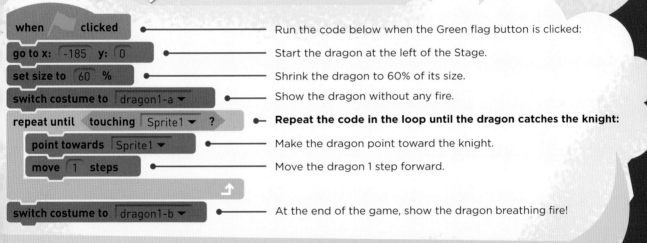

Run the code below when the Green flag button is clicked:

Start the dragon at the left of the Stage.

Shrink the dragon to 60% of its size.

Show the dragon without any fire.

Repeat the code in the loop until the dragon catches the knight:

Make the dragon point toward the knight.

Move the dragon 1 step forward.

At the end of the game, show the dragon breathing fire!

7. Finally, we'll set the backdrop for the Stage to show the outside of the Enchanted Castle.

Click the **Stage** icon.

Click **Choose backdrop from library**.

Choose **castle5**. Then click **OK**.

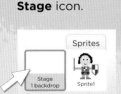

8. Click the **Green flag** to fly around on the magic carpet. Watch out for those flames!

Don't forget to save your game by clicking **File** then **Download to your computer**.

Escaping the dragon's flames, you land your flying carpet on the battlements. You descend a winding staircase into the gloom of the Enchanted Castle...

Ouch! Eeek! Help! Even the walls are attacking me!

Find Prince George and Princess Georgina quickly! But watch out for the...

ENCHANTED WALLS

1. Start a new Scratch file and **delete** the **cat sprite**.

2. Click the **Backdrops** tab.

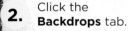

Select the **Fill** tool.

Click **light gray**.

Fill in the background by clicking on it.

3. We need to add some walls to the backdrop. (These walls will not move.)

Choose the **Brush** tool and select a **dark gray**.

Make the brush width a little **thicker**.

Draw a small brick outline.

Choose the **Fill** tool and select a **medium gray**.

Fill in the brick wall.

Draw **2** other brick walls in the same way.

When you have finished, your backdrop should look like this, with **3** small brick walls.

4. To add the prince, click the **Choose sprite from library** button.

Prince

Scroll down then click the **Prince** icon.

OK

Click **OK**.

5. Add the princess in the same way.

Princess

Scroll down then click the **Princess**.

OK

Click **OK**.

6. Click the **Shrink** button. Now **click** the **prince** and **princess** several times on the **Stage** until they are the same size as the walls.

7. Drag George and Georgina over to the **right** side of the Stage.

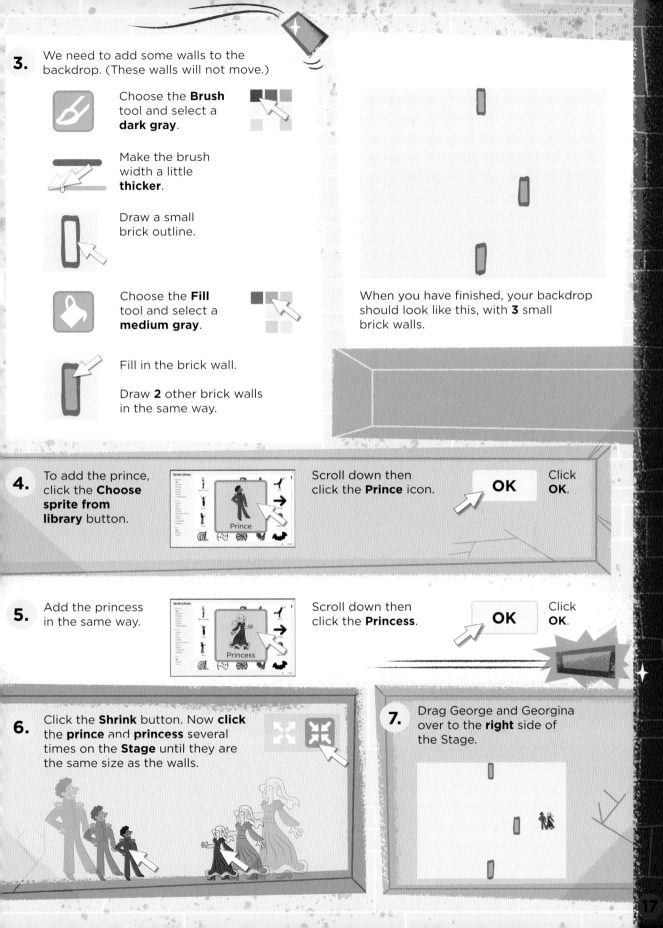

8.

Now upload your **knight** sprite.

Find your file and click **OK**.

9. Click the **Scripts** tab and drag this code to the **Scripts Area** to control the movement of the **knight**. For help with setting the color in the **"Touching color"** block, turn to page 12. All the other light blue blocks are also in the **Sensing** group. Use their drop-down menus to change the key.

Scripts

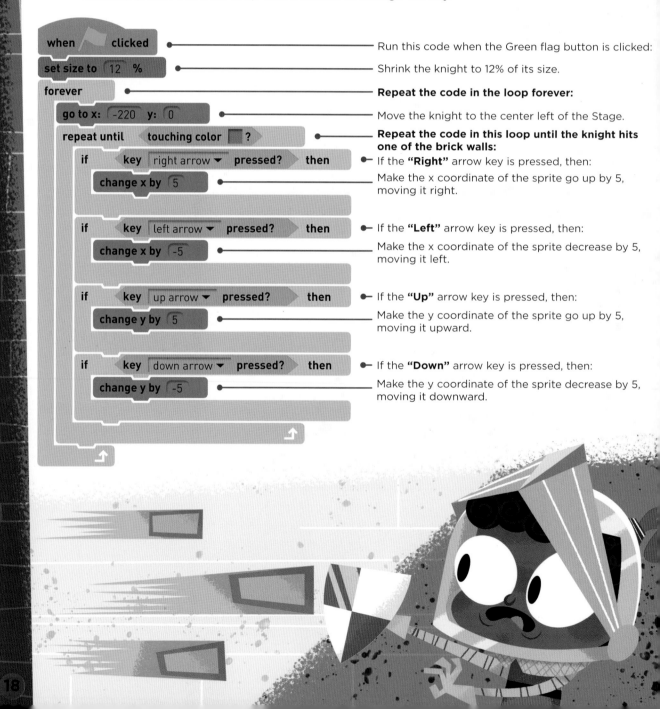

when [flag] clicked — Run this code when the Green flag button is clicked:

set size to 12 % — Shrink the knight to 12% of its size.

forever — **Repeat the code in the loop forever:**

go to x: -220 y: 0 — Move the knight to the center left of the Stage.

repeat until touching color [ ] ? — **Repeat the code in this loop until the knight hits one of the brick walls:**

if key right arrow ▼ pressed? then — If the **"Right"** arrow key is pressed, then:

change x by 5 — Make the x coordinate of the sprite go up by 5, moving it right.

if key left arrow ▼ pressed? then — If the **"Left"** arrow key is pressed, then:

change x by -5 — Make the x coordinate of the sprite decrease by 5, moving it left.

if key up arrow ▼ pressed? then — If the **"Up"** arrow key is pressed, then:

change y by 5 — Make the y coordinate of the sprite go up by 5, moving it upward.

if key down arrow ▼ pressed? then — If the **"Down"** arrow key is pressed, then:

change y by -5 — Make the y coordinate of the sprite decrease by 5, moving it downward.

10. Now we'll draw an enchanted wall sprite. It should have about **6 bricks** in it. Leave a **wide gap in the middle** so the knight can fit through.

Click **Paint new sprite**.

When finished, your wall drawing should be **almost the full height** of the Drawing Area. If not, the game might not work properly.

90%

Select the **Brush** and choose **dark gray**.

Draw the outline of **1** brick in the wall.

Draw **2** more bricks below it. Leave a gap, then draw **3** more bricks.

Choose **Fill** and **medium gray**.

Color in the bricks.

11. To make the **enchanted wall** sprite move, click the **Scripts** tab and drag this code to the **Scripts Area**.

Scripts

when 🏳 clicked — Run the code below when the Green flag button is clicked:

set size to 70 % — Shrink the enchanted wall sprite to 70% of its size.

set rotation style don't rotate ▼ —• Stop the wall from rotating when it changes direction.

point in direction 180 ▼ — Start by moving the wall downward.

forever — **Repeat the code in the loop forever:**

    if on edge, bounce — If the wall hits the edge of the Stage, bounce it back in the opposite direction.

    move 1 steps — Move the wall 1 step in the current direction.

12. Add another wall by **right clicking** the **wall** icon and choosing **Duplicate**.

info

duplicate

13. Drag the new wall into a space. Consider where to position your walls so you don't make the game too hard.

14. Click the **Green flag** to rescue the prince and princess!

Save your game by clicking **File** and **Download to your computer**.

Thank you for coming to rescue us! But you must defeat Wizard Malvin before any of us can escape this castle.

Malvin is hiding in the Dark Tower, guarded by his ghost knights. I kept my magic wand hidden from him. Take it so you can fight his magic with your own!

Sir Percival is shaking with fear! Can you battle the ghost knights and enter the Dark Tower alone?

THE DARK TOWER

1.   Start a new file and **delete** the **cat sprite**.

duplicate

delete

2. Click **Backdrops**.

Choose the **Fill** tool.

Choose **very dark blue**.

Fill in the background.

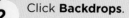 Scripts Backdrops

3. Choose the **Rectangle** tool. Select **black**, then click the **Solid rectangle**.

4. Draw the Dark Tower using rectangles.

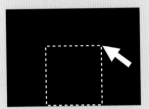   

Start with the base.   Add the battlements at the top.   Finish with the grass.

5. Upload your **knight** sprite. Click **Upload sprite from file**.

```
My Documents
game.sb2
knight.sprite2
maze.sb2
                    OK
```

Find your file and click **OK**.

 The sprite will appear.

6. We're going to use the knight quite small, so the sword it's holding will look like Georgina's magic wand! Let's add a flash of magic lightning to fire at the ghost knights from the wand.

Click **Choose sprite from library**.

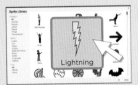 Scroll down then click the **Lightning**.

 OK Click **OK**.

7. Click the **Scripts** tab and drag these blocks into the **Scripts Area** for the lightning sprite. For the **"Go to sprite1"** block, choose the **"Go to mouse-pointer"** block then use the drop-down menu.

Scripts

when `space ▼` key pressed	●— Run the code below when the **"Space"** key is pressed:
show	●——— Make the lightning sprite visible.
set size to `5` %	●— Shrink the lightning to 5% of its size.
go to `Sprite1 ▼`	●— Move the lightning to the knight sprite.
repeat `20`	●— **Repeat the code in the loop 20 times:**
change y by `20`	●— Move the lightning up quickly, 20 steps at a time.

8.

To create a ghost knight, click **Choose sprite from library**.

Scroll down then click the **Knight** icon.

Knight

 **OK** Click **OK**.

9. Click the **Scripts** tab and drag these blocks into the **Scripts Area** for the **ghost knight**. We need to create lots of ghost knights. To do this we will use a special method called cloning, which duplicates sprites when the **"Create clone"** block runs. To make the **"Set ghost effect"** block, drag in a **"Set color effect"** block then use the drop-down menu to change it to **"ghost."**

Scripts

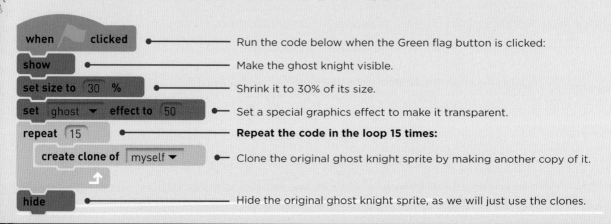

when 🏳 clicked	Run the code below when the Green flag button is clicked:
show	Make the ghost knight visible.
set size to 30 %	Shrink it to 30% of its size.
set ghost ▼ effect to 50	Set a special graphics effect to make it transparent.
repeat 15	**Repeat the code in the loop 15 times:**
create clone of myself ▼	Clone the original ghost knight sprite by making another copy of it.
hide	Hide the original ghost knight sprite, as we will just use the clones.

10. Now we will add code for each **ghost knight** clone. Drag this script **underneath** the code from step 9. It doesn't need to touch any of the previous code. The green **"Pick random"** block is in the **Operators** group. Drop it in the hole in the **"Set x to"** and **"Set y to"** blocks.

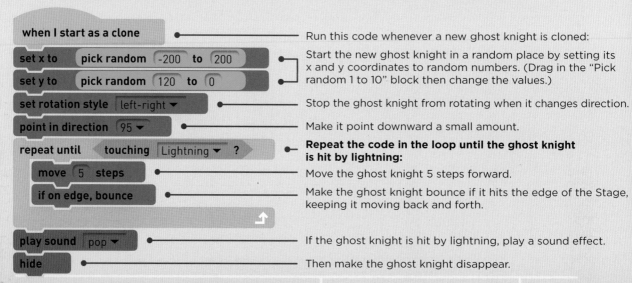

when I start as a clone	Run this code whenever a new ghost knight is cloned:
set x to pick random -200 to 200	Start the new ghost knight in a random place by setting its x and y coordinates to random numbers. (Drag in the "Pick random 1 to 10" block then change the values.)
set y to pick random 120 to 0	
set rotation style left-right ▼	Stop the ghost knight from rotating when it changes direction.
point in direction 95 ▼	Make it point downward a small amount.
repeat until touching Lightning ▼ ?	**Repeat the code in the loop until the ghost knight is hit by lightning:**
move 5 steps	Move the ghost knight 5 steps forward.
if on edge, bounce	Make the ghost knight bounce if it hits the edge of the Stage, keeping it moving back and forth.
play sound pop ▼	If the ghost knight is hit by lightning, play a sound effect.
hide	Then make the ghost knight disappear.

11. In the **Sprites Pane**, click on your **own knight** sprite. Then drag this code to the **Scripts Area**.

when 🏳 clicked	Run the code below when the Green flag button is clicked:
set size to 12 %	Shrink our own knight to 12% of its size.
go to x: 0 y: -140	Move our knight to the center bottom of the Stage.
wait until touching Knight2 ▾ ?	**Wait until our knight is hit by a ghost knight, then:**
say Agggh! for 2 secs	Show a message.
stop all ▾	Stop all the code from running, because the game is over!

12. Click the **Green flag** to battle with the ghost knights. Press the **"Space"** key to fire your magic lightning bolts at the ghost knights before they reach you and Sir Percival!

Remember to save your game by choosing **File** then **Download to your computer**.

You battle your way into the Dark Tower and come face to face with...WIZARD MALVIN!

HAAAA! So you think you can defeat ME! I have a challenge for you, little knight. Come into the dark woods and battle your magic against mine. If you beat me, I will release the prince and princess —and let you have my Book of Spells. Do you dare fight me?

How can you turn down a challenge like that? Get your magic wand ready!

WIZARD DUEL

1. Start a new Scratch file. **Delete** the **cat sprite**.

2. Let's create a spooky wood background.

Click the **Stage** icon.

Click **Choose backdrop from library**.

Choose **Woods**.

Then click **OK**.

3. To create Wizard Malvin, click **Choose sprite from library**.

Scroll down then click the **Wizard** icon.

OK Click **OK**.

4. Now we will add a star sprite from the library (for our magic spells).

Scroll down then click the **Star1** icon.

Click **OK**.

OK

5. Let's also give our knight a magic wand from the library.

Choose the **Magic wand** icon.

Click **OK**.

OK

6. Upload your **knight** sprite.

Click **Upload sprite from file**.

My Documents
game.sb2
knight.sprite2
maze.sb2

OK

Find your file and click **OK**.

The sprite will appear.

Sprite1

7. We will add some code to our **knight** sprite so the game ends if Malvin reaches the knight. Click the **Scripts** tab then drag these blocks into the **Scripts Area**.

Scripts

when [flag] clicked — Run the code below when the Green flag button is clicked:

set size to 20 % — Shrink the knight to 20% of its size.

wait until touching Wizard ? — **Wait until the knight has been attacked by Wizard Malvin, then:**

say Aggghhh! for 2 secs — Show a message.

stop all — Stop all the code from running, because the game is over!

8. Now we will swap the knight's sword for Georgina's magic wand.

Costumes

In the center of the screen, click the **Costumes** tab.

Use the **Eraser** to rub out the knight's sword.

9. Click the **Green flag** to run the code. It will make your knight sprite shrink.

Then drag the **knight** sprite over to the **right side** of the Stage by the trees. Drag the **magic wand** sprite onto the knight's arm.

10. In the **Sprites Pane**, click the **magic wand** icon. Click the **Scripts tab**, then drag this code into the **Scripts Area**. It will allow you to move the wand to aim it at Wizard Malvin.

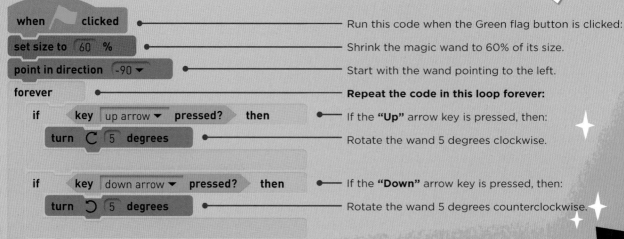

when 🏳 clicked ——————————— Run this code when the Green flag button is clicked:

set size to 60 % ——————————— Shrink the magic wand to 60% of its size.

point in direction -90 ▾ ——————————— Start with the wand pointing to the left.

forever ——————————— **Repeat the code in this loop forever:**

  if key up arrow ▾ pressed? then ——— If the **"Up"** arrow key is pressed, then:

    turn ↻ 5 degrees ——————————— Rotate the wand 5 degrees clockwise.

  if key down arrow ▾ pressed? then ——— If the **"Down"** arrow key is pressed, then:

    turn ↺ 5 degrees ——————————— Rotate the wand 5 degrees counterclockwise.

11. In the **Sprites Pane**, click the **star** icon. Drag these two separate chunks of code into the **Scripts Area**. They will control how the spell moves across the screen when you press the "Space" key to cast it.

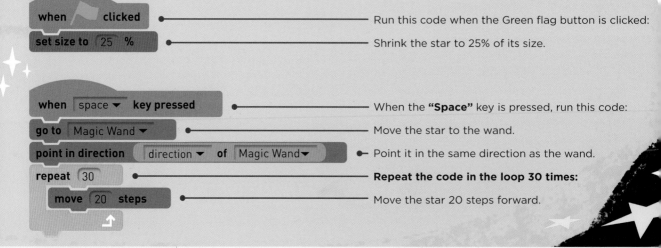

when 🏳 clicked ——————————— Run this code when the Green flag button is clicked:

set size to 25 % ——————————— Shrink the star to 25% of its size.

when space ▾ key pressed ——————————— When the **"Space"** key is pressed, run this code:

go to Magic Wand ▾ ——————————— Move the star to the wand.

point in direction direction ▾ of Magic Wand ▾ —— Point it in the same direction as the wand.

repeat 30 ——————————— **Repeat the code in the loop 30 times:**

  move 20 steps ——————————— Move the star 20 steps forward.

 direction ▾ of Magic Wand

Need help finding this code block?

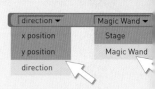

| Sensing

Choose the **Sensing** group.

x position ▾ of Magic Wand ▾

Scroll down to near the end of the group to find this block.

point in direction [x position ▾]

Drag it by the left corner and drop it into the **"Point in direction"** code block.

Choose **Direction**.

Choose **Magic wand**.

26

12. In the **Sprites Pane**, click the **wizard** icon. Drag these code blocks into the **Scripts Area**.

```
when [flag] clicked
set size to 70 %
repeat 20
    go to x: -200 y: pick random -160 to 160
    point towards Sprite1 ▼
    repeat until touching Star1 ▼ ?
        move 2 steps
    change ghost ▼ effect by 5
    play sound pop ▼
say You have defeated the wizard!
```

Run this code when the Green flag is clicked:

Shrink the wizard to 70% of its size.

Repeat the code in the loop 20 times:

Start the wizard in a random place on the left side of the Stage.
Point the wizard toward your knight.

Repeat until the wizard is hit by the spell (star):

Move the wizard 2 steps forward.

Make the wizard more transparent each time it is hit.
Play a sound effect when the wizard is hit.

Show a message—your spells have done the job!

13. Use the **arrow keys** on your keyboard to aim, then press the **"Space"** key to fire your spells. Every time you hit Malvin, he will get weaker. Keep going until he disappears!

Don't forget to save your game by choosing **File** then **Download to your computer**.

Aaaaaargh! You are beating me, little knight!

> **NOOOO! You shall not have my Book of Spells!**

Wizard Malvin rips up the Book of Spells before disappearing with a puff of smoke. Quick! Dodge the thunderbolts and pick up all 50 pages of the book.

THE BOOK OF SPELLS

1. 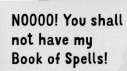 Start a new Scratch file and **delete** the **cat sprite**.

2. Click **Backdrops**.

Choose the **Fill** tool and pick **dark purple**.

Fill in the background.

3. Now upload your **knight** sprite by clicking **Upload sprite from file**.

4. We need to count how many pages have been collected. We will use a variable. Variables are a way that computer programs store values that can change—such as the score.

Sound
Pen
Data

Make a Variable

Variable name: [Pages]

OK

Click the **Data** group.   Click **Make a variable**.   Call it **Pages**.   Then click **OK**.

5. To draw a sprite for the thunderbolt, click the **Paint new sprite** button.

The thunderbolt should be about **half the width** of the Drawing Area.

50%

Choose **yellow** and select the **Line** tool.

Make the line **thicker**.

Draw the outline of the thunderbolt.

Choose **Fill** and color in the thunderbolt.

6. Click the **Scripts** tab and drag these blocks into the **Scripts Area** to control the **thunderbolt**.

Scripts

```
when       clicked
set size to  20  %
forever
    go to x:  -220  y:  150
    point towards  Sprite1 ▼
    repeat until    touching  edge ▼  ?
        move  5  steps
```

Run the code below when the Green flag button is clicked:

Shrink the thunderbolt to 20% of its size.

Repeat the code in the loop forever:

Move the thunderbolt to the top left of the Stage.

Point the thunderbolt toward the knight.

Repeat the code in this loop until the thunderbolt hits the edge of the Stage:

Move the thunderbolt 5 steps forward.

7. In the **Sprites Pane**, click on the **knight** sprite. Then click on the **Scripts** tab and drag these blocks into the **Scripts Area** to control your knight.

Sprite1

```
when       clicked
set  Pages ▼  to  0
set size to  20  %
set rotation style  don't rotate ▼
go to x:  220  y:  -120
repeat until    touching color  □  ?
    point towards  mouse-pointer ▼
    move  2  steps

say  AGGGHHHH! ▼
```

Run the code below when the Green flag button is clicked:

At the start, set the count of pages collected to zero.

Shrink the knight to 20% of its size.

Stop the knight from rotating as it moves around the Stage.

Start the knight at the bottom right of the Stage.

Repeat the code in the loop until the knight is hit by a (yellow) thunderbolt (turn to page 12 for help with setting the color):

Point the knight toward the mouse.

Move the knight 2 steps forward.

If hit by a thunderbolt, scream!

8. Now we will draw a page in the Book of Spells. Click **Paint new sprite**.

The page should be about **half the height** of the Drawing Area.

Choose **white** and select the **Rectangle** tool.

Click to draw a **Solid rectangle**.

Draw a rectangle.

Choose **black** and select the **Text** tool.

Click in the rectangle.

Type the spell of your choice.

9. Click the **Scripts** tab and drag these two separate chunks of code into the **Scripts Area**. The first one creates 50 cloned pages. The second one tells each cloned page what to do.

Scripts

when [flag] clicked —————————— Run the code below when the Green flag button is clicked:

set size to (20) % —————————— Shrink the page to 20% of its size.

show ————————————————— Make sure the page is visible.

repeat (50) ———————————— **Repeat the code in the loop 50 times:**

    create clone of [myself ▼] ——— Clone the original page sprite by making a copy of it.

hide ————————————————— Hide the original page, as we just need the clones.

when I start as a clone ——————— When a new clone is made, run this code:

go to [random position ▼] ———— Move the cloned page to a random place on the Stage.

repeat (pick random (1) to (10)) —— **Repeat this code a few times (between 1 and 10 times):**

    turn ↻ (15) degrees —————— Spin the cloned page around 15 degrees.

wait until (touching [Sprite1 ▼] ?) —— **Wait until the knight collects the page (touches it).**

change [Pages ▼] by (1) ———— Then add 1 to the count of collected pages.

play sound [pop ▼] ——————— Play a sound effect.

hide ————————————————— Hide the cloned page, because it has been collected.

10. Now click the **Green flag** button. Move your **mouse pointer** to direct the knight sprite. Watch the score go up as you collect the pages.

Don't forget to save your game!

GLOSSARY

Clone – One or more copies of a Scratch sprite. Cloning is used to create multiple sprites quickly.

Code – A series of instructions or commands.

Command – A word or code block that tells the computer what to do.

Coordinates – The position of an object determined by its x (center to right) and y (center to top) values.

Data group – The set of Scratch code blocks that control and access variables.

Degree – The unit measuring the angle that an object turns.

Drawing Area – The part of the right-hand side of the Scratch screen that is used to draw sprites and backgrounds.

Duplicate – A simple way to create a copy of a sprite in Scratch.

Events group – The set of Scratch code blocks that are triggered when particular events happen, such as a key being pressed.

If then – A common form of selection in coding, where command(s) are run if something is true.

Language – A system of commands (in the form of blocks, words, or numbers) that tell a computer how to do things.

Loop – A sequence of code blocks repeated a number of times.

Operators group – The set of Scratch code blocks that deals with calculations and comparing values.

Program – The set of commands that tell a computer how to do something such as play a game.

Scratch – A computer language that uses blocks of code to make a program.

Scripts Area – The part of the right-hand side of the Scratch screen to which code blocks are dragged to create programs.

Sensing group – The set of Scratch code blocks that detect when specific keys are pressed or where the mouse is.

Speed – How fast an object moves forward. In Scratch, we use minus speed values to move objects backward.

Sprite – An object that moves around the screen.

Sprites Pane – Part of the lower left of the Scratch screen where you select a sprite to add code to or change its appearance.

Stage – The area at the top left of the Scratch screen where you can watch your sprites move.

Variable – A value or piece of information stored by a computer program. In computer games, a variable is commonly used to store the score.

INDEX